One Eternal Sleep

Bill F. Ndi

Langaa Research & Publishing CIG
Mankon, Bamenda

Publisher:
Langaa RPCIG
Langaa Research & Publishing Common Initiative Group
P.O. Box 902 Mankon
Bamenda
North West Region
Cameroon
Langaagrp@gmail.com
www.langaa-rpcig.net

Distributed in and outside N. America by African Books Collective
orders@africanbookscollective.com
www.africanbookscollective.com

ISBN: 9956-792-31-4

© Bill F. Ndi 2015

DISCLAIMER
All views expressed in this publication are those of the author and do not necessarily reflect the views of Langaa RPCIG.

Dedication

To my beloved Brother and sister: Samuel Sunday Ndi, (Rested in the Lord on January 24th 2013) and Reverend Magdalene Mbutngah Ndi who lived and Rested in the Lord and in His service on August 16th 2014. Peace unto their souls and to God Almighty be the Glory for their lives.

Table of Contents

Review vii

For Brother Sunny: Rested in the Lord on
January 24th 2013 1
Ni Sunny *(Pulera Jumai NDI,)* 2
When I'm done! 3
Victory is Won 4
Where the Circle Starts 5
Buried Gloom 6
RIP Ni Sunny 7
No Tears to Bury Me 8
The New Reign 9
Fiends' Woes 10
Chimerical Fame 11
The Throes of Canal Gasp 12
His strife to fight 13
Smooth Transition 14
Farewell 15
Farewell II 16
Farewell III 17
Farewell IV 18
Farewell V 19
Farewell VI 20
Farewell VII 21
Farewell VIII 22
Mining Joy 23
Live My Love 24
Hit the Sky 25
Down the Pits 26

Imp Patience..27
About Man..28
Comrade Digger..29
Goodbye Reveler...30
Hunched..31
Game me not...32
Franc & Deception..33
Salesman of Ignorance..................................34
Flirts and the Greedy Sea..............................35
The Liar..36
Ink in Our Vein...37
Brother to Sister..38
Our Clime & Crime......................................39
Apostrophe..40
That Game..41
Off the Hook...42
Trap I won't Fall in..43
Election...44
Devotees..45
My Journey Home...46
Only Their Reality...47
Completing the circle....................................48
Here Comes the Clown.................................49
Unwanted in my Resting Place.....................50
Ebola...51
Drum by the Grave.......................................52

Review

In this collection Bill F. Ndi challenges his readers' sense of the human reality all call death. We have all been taken unawares by death and reduced to groaning, moaning, and mourning. But should this be? The poet persists in blurring the boundaries between life and death. For him, by dying, life does seem to shift from the higher grounds to the lower grounds and/or vice-versa. The communion of life and death to Bill F. Ndi is but a blissful marriage made in heaven which only the misinformed mind conceives to be a marriage of incompatible elements from hell.

Also, for Bill F. Ndi, the beginning of life, which is the beginning of the cultivation of knowledge, i.e. death, is never too soon. Yet, paradoxically, mortals torture themselves to a thousand deaths before their deaths simply because death visits them, knocks at their doors and welcomes home one of theirs. Such mortals would bewail and curse *in fine* and accusing death for having come too soon forgetting all along, death has been there with them since birth. Hence the poet's challenge to the reader to quest why the reader never considers his/her coming too soon, yet, views the going so.

For Brother Sunny: Rested in the Lord on January 24th 2013

Dear brother, since you left
Not a day leaves us deaf
To your gentle heart beat
That with love beat, it beat
To the rhythm of love
We hadn't enough of
And death came to stop you
Not in our hearts where you
On the throne of love sit
And decry death, misfit
Full of hopes we would cry
Crying to see you die
But we are of God's stock
And accept God's love struck
You and you would not heed
Our will but take the lead
For 'twas our Father's will
Yours came to a standstill.

RIP Sunny Boy
Keep shining Sunny Boy

Ni Sunny *(by Pulera Jumai NDI)*

Dear brother cum brother
In-law I'd not bother
After I'm with crying done,
Death that may kill
Would never, never kill
You, our only True LOVE!
On a Valentine's Day?
Granted! You're gone to stay
In your new home above
Far from sounds of a gun
And are by doves greeted.
They spread us your gifted
Heavenly prize for peace
You'd worked for without fees;
Now in our depth you bloom
And inter death's gloom
Away from bosom hearts
Here crowded by your hearth!

02/14/2013

When I'm done!

When I'm done playing my drum
I'd not want a taste of rum
For it's not been the favorite
After which I ever cried
Were it your favorite, I'd give
A sea of rum to relief
You of pain not 'cos I'm gone;
My parting breaks but this dawn
And on you it dawns what life
In its store would we as strife
Had to run around the like
Of children riding their bike
With no one to beat them drums
Or beat them as you do the scums.

02/16/2013

Victory is won

The day we accepted to be born
Was the same day we our victory won
Over death who would she marked an end
To this life we now savor and trend
Knowing we'll need to go and roost home
Not before we have the crannies combed
Elsewhere, we have laughed and should laugh
For death is nothing but a riffraff
Gloating with sole joy to still our joy
A thing that should not make us coy.
With our quintessence immaterial,
To her we give all the material
Laughingly as we know our essence
Present with our material absence.

02/26/13

Where the Circle Starts

It was in death that Christ brought life
So shall all in death regain life
'Cos for a seed to grow, it must
Rot. Rot? Humans shan't when they trust
In their maker for recycle
And go to complete their cycle
As human life is just one stage
Of that to be written on his page
Let us go when it is time and waste
No time; it would leave a bitter taste
In mouths designed to savor pleasure
And glorify the future treasure
Promised to the upright and forthright
In a world void of everything plight.

02/26-03/11/13

Buried Gloom

Beneath the gilded smiles of clowns
Sits such rosy misery that crowns
The thorny life of oblivious
Men for whom ache isn't obvious
And has them radiate foolishness
Flagging faith in God sheepishness
Which sheepishness aft them, they fail
To see, trail the like of a tail
Leaving a giant tale to our friends
Who with jollity ward off fiends
And make us our troubles forget
Till the day we without a jet
Take off to soar above the clouds
Where our bright lit smiles form our shrouds.

02/26/13

RIP Ni Sunny

Sunny is not dead
Sunny's known rebirth
And shall never die.
He's just lifted high
To be with the most
High in whom, the most
He believes does shield
In all battle field
Where humans seek love
And still find it rough
Yet, leaving us
Sunny has shown us
There's no refuge
But God's Love so huge!

02/25/2013

No Tears to Bury Me

He wipes my tears when I cry
And shall comfort me when I die
So, why waste your time with these cries
When I live and have died in Christ?
I know him flesh, bone and spirit
Thought of as waste on which to spit
By foes who themselves fool ten folds
Chanting my name Stupid in bolds.
Stupid? Yes! I'd rather be one
Such lamb whose meekness is taken
Out of sheepishness for self-pride,
They joy I would have for a ride
But my calm I'd keep right up-front
And not snake around with a grunt.

The New Reign

At the funeral, thousands of voices
Praised and raised the dead against vices
Heaped on him when alive, all in hope
He'd sink in the deeps t' emerge high on dope.
Yet, heaven broke open for the light to stream
And suck him into this eternal realm
Where at home, he begins an all new reign
Far from that craved by the world in its drain.
Beautiful realm, realm of bliss, dreamless realm
Whereby the Master alone steers the helm
And by which Master come my time I'd sleep
Peacefully, profound and baby deep sleep.
When it comes to pass, all shall be well
And will leave many a story to tell.

Fiends' Woes

At home ours would stimulate a new reign
In which heartbeats do not with sorrows rain
But beat to send sounds to fiends strapped in woes
And tempest that of them doth make scarecrows
On a trail blazed for them by they themselves
With willful choice to be led by same elves
Whose now shattered thoughts fed both cats and crows
Who the farmer's plight took for a smidgeon
Doomed to be cast as scuff in a dungeon
Down the ravening and burning bellies
Out of which toxic and lethal lie flies
Into these eardrums like arrows from bows
Only this new homecoming king would stop
And have us lose not even a teardrop.

Chimerical Fame

I look at the sky and seek where it ends
When I probe into life in which one fends
For no end, I know it shan't be the same
At the end when we bid farewell to fame
Fame which swells men's head above and beyond
The shame with which Man would he kept a bond;
Ere, I falter, such fame shall never last
Not even when it fools it gives a blast.
As I plod, I need not seek but my end
To come with my name none would ever bend
For it is the only to perish
Were I to live and treat it like a dish;
To eat, digest, excrete and turn away
From it with haste that links me not that way.

The Throes of Canal Gasp

When it is our time to drop down the chips
We'll have just that to do without giving tips
And would not need to cry over spilled milk
Had we our life's journey transformed to silk
Whose finesse outmatches, for the mundane,
Bliss marked by shimmering mirage that is vain
And driven home by thoughtless brain in quest
Of things to be left when we must take our rest
Rest which must a stop put to carnal gasp
Quick to grab than spirit game we must grasp.
In our quest for victory in the spirit
We must stop to think of Him as of it
For He shapes our world and casts it between
Light and darkness sharing one birth like twins.

His strife to fight

Now that you have come I will rather go
And be free from the chains of this mean foe;
Though my love would see him shriek at your sight
Come his day, for I know he'd strive to fight
For, he never such a day envisioned
Ignoring you had us all positioned
To take turns to host you after our stay
Here is close; caring not who made who prey.
Predators sought the preys to gain long life
Just as my kind to the foe for their life.
Now, with nature I would rest without doubt
As I gladly stay away from the crowd,
No, gang of thieves to which these lords belong
And attack kindred with their two-pronged tongue.

Smooth Transition

Death can only kill when we negate life
And would we rather slice it with a knife
As if it were a piece of cake to eat
And not the follow up of the spirit
Which beyond sentient thoughts blooms and blossoms
With bubbles of mirth filled laughs in bosoms
Not hidden but buxom and in plain sight
Tickling the mind and shielding it from fight
Worthless fight cowards die for, oftentimes
Yet with death's lull I would not heed the chimes
And sparkles that blind, deafen and still her
Not when I know life to be sweet… sweeter,
No 'tis the sweetest for all to embrace
And leave man's transition needing no brace.

Farewell

It was April, I last saw daddy!
Dad was about to leave his body
In hospital bed! He took my hand
Which he squeezed and squeezed hard with his hand
And mused we'd scream out loud in August!
I dreamt we'd with joy do come August!
Then he entered me as I was blank
Knowing not come August he'd be plank
And have our tears wash the stele
He'd have us erect with none to feel
That August of my nativity
Be August of his mortality.
Yet, both death and birth come August
I thus embrace the two as life's trust!

12/09/10

Farewell II

My hand? Dad gripped hard never to let go!
And when I left he knew he had to go!
And left words behind for a wanderer
Who'd so become come early September
When a new ridge would grace with awe the piece
Given him to administer in Peace
And call all heads to drop as they pass by
In this journey for which they would not vie
Now I know the ultimate end of time
So close that one never gets to its prime
By our own measure by which we assume
In plenty we have nothing to consume
The infiniteness of it though finite
With more than half spent with our tears glossed plight.

19/09/10

Farewell III

Down there, daddy is strong and carries
All by himself, an obelisk that's his
And tells his story as a soldier
Who fought a fight, though not a ranger,
With his wisdom to kids to challenge
Their anger with calm void of revenge
And such spirit that would invite war;
From which lessons he would all one draw
To grace this world with calm known at night
When the world does in deep sleep alight.
From a distant land I grieve and stroke
Daddy's obelisk and would he woke
Up to have these words his eyes caress
Before he takes this prolong recess…!

10/04/10

Farewell IV

I'd have liked to think 'twas just a bad dream
Made me plunge in love like kids in a stream
Just to find it was nothing but lava
Destined to burn up any who lover
Professes they were just to wake up in
This river with venom full to the bream!
Is Love worth dying for, thus worth living
For in spite of the mask worn by lying
Hussies who keep off dents and dints from brave
And honest hearts they would make of their slave?
True! Life reserves surprises that abound
But not the odium that would love drag aground
Bound to that bad dream of my thoughts I hate
Here present that others muse on as fate.

17-20/10/10

Farewell V

My eyes dropped in a pit six feet deep
Dad's remains welcomed them not a death sheep
Yet, my life source does prick the eyes so hard
Me in want with my mouth drooped wide a yard!
Rocked by this pit's content, thrown in a feat,
I here on these grounds miss the grain of wheat
And hope for rebirth and bloom far afield
By a grave in which none ever needs a shield
Long after these eyes on the man did feast
With no thoughts of the fate of man nor beast
Where one drives home tears, the other relish
Not tear that's brought by famine but anguish
As fallen eyes in the pit remedy
Not needles grown at heart by tragedy.

Farewell VI

Dad would not speak nor sing; he only mused
As he shipped himself out with none amused.
I turn my ears to his musings to hear
Them project in this ride one needs no fear
Just as he'd done to teach to write on slates
That our ends should shake no tectonic plates
But take heed this were a gentle motion
To a land so still with no commotion,
Remote from this, where our hairs stand on strands
Safe when we take a goner down with bands
Drumming him goodbye while he lies down mute
After he's quit this world of disrepute
A shroud covers the little ones he'd taught
To drop their hats and face the draught he'd brought.

Farewell VII

I thought I'd rather not think dad this year.
Twenty one years gone! His voice? I still hear
Shining the light on my way to wisdom
By which dad swore would serve my kind freedom;
The one I await to bloom and blossom
In their jail house while they squeeze out ransom.
Just before daddy jumped out of his bag
To me, he brandished their sleazy filthy rag
And ignited this quest for refinement
That has turned me away from deployment
And have my eyes open to tranquility
To front their rage with equanimity
For my calm never to know privation
But, how to inhale breath of liberation.

Farewell VIII

Can I bury this image on my mind?
How come? Not even when to truth blind?
He'd strained his waist to lay my foundation
Erect and tall with pride to see me born
With spring sprout brought by me, winged cherub
To his heart whose beats resound with a throb.
As he would he went, my own starts to beat
Fast with rage for a parting dad so sweet.
Yes, he's been the nectar with me the bee
Who tapped joy from his buds and drank sweet tea!
Now, he's gone with the source of my tears left
To flood my cheeks as my cry tells of theft
That broke this dam forcing questions to stream
Out. Yet, my heart knows it should with joy scream!

Mining Joy

With tears at dawn, he's unable to cope
With a taste of disobedience like dope
He'd had all day day long to kill pain
In which his heartbeats with joyfulness rain,
They rain the misery he now has to wear
Whence he could have braved the pain without fear;
Fear without which cowards will never die
And with their death I ask: why should one cry?
Take not my quest for numbness of a heart
For mine beat hard and fast like tennis bat
Striking the ball to fall on the table
Edge to birth forth joy so memorable
Only a tear of the disenfranchised
Would have my heart that mines destabilized.

Live My Love

For my love I would I lived
For my love they would I died
For my love I say no to die
My back against them knots their tie
The one with which they'd make a noose
As I wax strong the like of moose
In the woods where wolves do feed
On remnants of those whose need
To see me deed killed them all
With me alone upright and tall
With chocolate brown they live not
To see my iron tree wrought
Not with human hands man sees
But those which from above frees.

Hit the Sky

When we take pride in pride, what shall the end,
Reserved for us, other than bee sting, be?
With on our heads loads of the rules they bend
And entwine to keep us from being free;
Freedom dream like Langston's won't be a fight
Deferred; for here on earth we must enjoy
And take pleasure of this absolute Right
With which power tricksters would like to toy
And leave us locking horns the like of rams
Far from the rights we must not with arms
Fight for. In vain attempt they would all stall
And force us within those walls filled with gall;
With which gall they would not catch any fly
For we're therein with wings and choice to fly.

Down the Pits

To adult entertain me for laughter
By the vales of Sodom and Gomorrah
A pal with urge to turn me on, my tears'
Tap opened and let bleed the fears one hears;
Far from feasting the eyes and standing up
Tall and erect, jitters flooded my spine
As I came to sight a world so corrupt
To pull fallen seraphs to stand in line
And feast on such nakedness here on earth
By the foe placed forth with will to bring dearth;
Guild, and propel in that want for carnal
Man's bliss, one so blind to see beyond now
And all that which clings to the physical
And steals away all thoughts of tomorrow.

Imp Patience

Your might has been seen digging deep for gold
Where your weakness leaves man to be the mold
And that's where your might should have been so bold
Now, like Sisyphus you push your madness
Uphill and wish to turn blind to sadness
Running naked to sniff of nothingness
In your magma pavements for which payments
Let fall water droplets of bereavement
That give you, ghoul your heart's fulfillment
As you see some men succumb to your weight
Especially those who fall for your bait
For their impatience spurs them not to wait
Where our likes burn with zeal to stand still
And welcome a life marked by a higher Will

About Man

At the center? No rho!
A woman with a hoe
And a litter
And so bitter
On whom and on which
From without man's wish
An Eye away from such groats
Roams, Roves, and Gloats,
As his mouth waters,
As his body jitters,
As his member nods
With mad thoughts
Of nakedness
Raging around nakedly reckless.

Comrade Digger

I caught a glimpse of a comrade digging
The grave of he who ours has been digging
For long rope years now drawing to an end
As we have chosen life and would defend
Ours from his breed of hyenas-wolves-vultures
Who would rather make sure we were manures
To fertilize their imagined nation;
So the other side of our own notion
Of a nation with life full to the bream
Just as would a stream that gives one to bream.
Dig comrade dig for us to make muddy
With our tears, the tomb you for him ready!
Widen his big, the size of our broad smile
For such is a fit hat for the senile.

Goodbye Reveler

Come not wailing when amusement your cup
Fills full with sadness sweeps that have them drop
As my eye caught you in the throes of bliss
Masochistically reveling the squeeze
That would their breathing stop for they did sound
Notes so fiery that would rock ships aground.
Why not let such song makers rest in peace
After you have made away with their fleece
And dispossess us well of the golden
Sound that they send to come and embolden
Many a somnolent soul in stupor;
Your dream come-true people to lord over
For, you do pray these souls live and be poor
Yet, their farewell they bid you forever.

Hunched

I was told the monster lives in Zimbabwe
And was intimated his name is Mugabe
A lie wrapped in a bouquet of warped message
Shoved down my throat as if giving a massage
To relieve me of some fatal strain of pain
And I feel the weight of their lies on my brain
Resurge my agony as their stab jags in
To put me down with spasmodic twinge within.
Pain, pain, go away! Take your ache and go
And spare me your trouble; let me your lies throw
Away and bathe in the pool devoid of blood
Stained lies served to many of my kind at odd
With thorny truth, so prickly to be reframed
All because the chum refuses to be tamed.

Game me not

Point your gun to my skull and post your smile
In your face, I'll tell you you're infantile
For my skull is home to substance grey in color
Too strong to let torture leave him in dolor
As no cloud would get him cloudier than grey
Not even when with loots you would you pay
To dull the cranial substance I bow to
And to which you push your folly far up
And prop cranks and punks ready to say stop
To such leaves that hold drops of morning dew
In our land you claim yours and would leave dry
For us to wail while you heed not our cry;
Walled in your life sentence presidency,
Stench filled latrine devoid of decency.

Franc & Deception

That country lied and asked me to bid her
Adieu; unfit to drink from the fountain
That of truth by which I am pure fresh heir
Not their own sat here by those fame villains
Whose hexagonal dwelling bred black code
For my kind for whom none cared for the tongue
I wag is neither that of frog nor toad.
Must we always croak and behind them throng?
Now, I have to be Frank not like their franc;
Both father and mother of deception
Here unveiled for the stench of their rancid bank
To repel all with thoughts of reception
Liar country, leave my kind to their drink
As with my kind I will maintain this link.

Salesman of Ignorance

Never shall I glory at the death
Of a living dead whose moral dearth
Reeks the putridity of a corpse
Whose return to the soil would kill crops
Which in life he'd rather see abroad
Far off from where he the greenbacks hoard
Knowing not they shall outlast his sham
Bottled for fame to leave the poor ram
Without a Shepherd to herd the sheep
He takes my people for down the deep
Where he is lord of the underworld
And, would pass on to their intestines twirled
Pangs as their only certainty known to all
He wishes to see on their belly crawl.

Flirts and the Greedy Sea

Like a kid in a candy store, those folks
Gravitate around anything brand name;
Dependence on their slaver evokes
And injects thoughts of how the dark days came
And went without any seeing him pass
With such imposed brain function at its best
Flirting with such old greedy sea whose test
Does nothing but gives takers an impasse
The bloom that once was the fate of my kind
Whose choice to head the herd was so unkind
To show all but that which folks ought to know
In their dark heart of double blinded scum
In some money trap wherein they'll not grow
And would have to spice up their life with rum.

The Liar

The cutting edge of a blade tells big lies
It is the sharpest whence it can't cut flies
Thrown in disarray by truth's cutting edge
This is where liars flock in with a masked pledge
Disparaging truth as the sledge hammer
That would shatter into bits and splinter
That which their eyes and thoughts behold as flags
Fanning hurricanes to sweep away rags;
These rags in which we are, with gaiety, clad
Incite, spin and propel all of them mad
When and as hurricanes come to a halt
And the soldiers' wages are paid in salt
And our lots carried by Mexican waves
Rehearse what a scarecrow, in the farm, craves.

Ink in Our Vein

Fill our veins oh Lord! Not with blood
But with ink that would cut like sword
When it strikes a sheet of paper
And leaves scars that prick like pepper
All those who in life nursed our plight
With us far away from their sight
They'll have to dance to the music
They'd intoned to pull us their trick.
With our blood stain omnipresent
We'll then look up for the crescent
To grow and blow their minds open
To the stabbed wound left by our pen
They had taken for child's play
For they thought they'd lead us astray.

Brother to Sister

Sister, sister your rose blooms inward
And glues my eyes on your outward
Buxom bosom that rinses them,
Cleans and places them at the helm
Wherein you drive me to safety
With tender strokes of a surety
That brings home the reassurance
I would sniff your sugary fragrance
Stirring my empire of senses
Not to run around for census
As there is one and only one
Sister with whose absence I'm wan
And from your source, my thirst, I'd quench
And won't need to fight in the trench.

Our Clime & Crime

The love we have for our crime
Is one that won't die with time
Would spark star readers' envy
Such that they'd make a levy
For you deprive me of sleep
And sheepishly like a sheep
I follow the trail you blaze
With a pen I use as brace
That upsets manmade muzzle
And leave man with a puzzle
That emit smells that make rhyme
That chimes in the ear our clime
And tide do just what they do.
And us? At best what we do.

Apostrophe

Death, didn't you know you're such a coward?
Your spirit came to say he's your steward
And when the nail pricked this palm and the blood
Dropped, he dashed out of our sight like an odd
Cloud the day after rainfall with new life
Brought to bear upon this earth where we strive
To paste a smile on faces you sadden
In your feat of a brazen and drunken
Clown in attempt to snatch and wear a crown
Not that of thorns left for us on the cross
Ignoring our sorrows in His blood drown
As this cross in our life is but a plus
On our shoulders as we our sojourn make,
A load that makes our life sugary sweet cake.

That Game

Refine your fun and make my kind graveyard
Residents; a stunt you shan't pull a yard
For my eyes glow with light years to expose
Your barbaric acts topped with overdose
Grooming your crave to see me fed fat on
A nightmare by which I stand and won't run
And would before your own face laugh out loud,
Feast my eyes on you getting the hell out
With your birthèd nightmare, a mere knave
Blowing but hot air that can't burn the brave
Molded by the Hands at the origin
Of this mirth, smile and laughter not the grin
You wear to see my kind off to churchyard
Which grin to crumple calls for a true bard.

Off the Hook

I'd pulled my neck from the hooks of this world
To ready my one way journey homeward
For what else is in my sac of bone, flesh
And blood if not the dusty truth so, fresh?
The wisdom of the Ancient of days says
This homecoming shall be clad in fine lace
And brightened by fine ray stream from His Heart
Man flags his coxcomb to and chops apart
For He beat the drum and rhythm of truth
To astound that of this world so uncouth.
In my journey mundane and rabid hounds,
Barking to make their mark with empty sounds
None would need at journey's end in deep sleep,
Show their fangs to my foot they cannot sweep.

Trap I won't Fall in

Fill your vial full with the bilious content
In hope my laden heart makes you content
Yet, your venture I embrace as fair play
And would cast my vote to cheer as the way
For by so doing I will stir your bile
And will terrorize your evil on file
That has borne the fruits none can his stomach
Fill with as would with piano strokes of Bach
Who with body and soul took to music
And bang keyboards to command artistic
Beauty and make our souls and hearts to pound
With joy that yours shall not drag to the ground.
Now, our hearts' vales full with the harmonic
Would not fall into your sick trap of trick.

Election

I elect cheerfulness to pave my way
Where the world would with stolidity pay
As recompense for my want to see all
With delight up erect and standing tall
Dressed in such a smile weathering affects not
Visible from a distance like a yacht
Cruising close to, and stroking our coastline
Radiating with and reflecting sunshine
We would in dire strait be, deprived of.
My choice to heighten my Spirit with love
Toughens and makes me impervious too
 And to this nature I will remain true
To be armed with weapons to hack their craze
Twenty thousand sanctified nights and days.

Devotees

Dip the pen deep in the ink
This one of devotedness
And hear a nightingale sing
Affection and loveliness
That would drive in you no pain
And you would see the pen stain
Spotless a sheet of paper
Which stain would prick like pepper
The eyes of those devotees
With dogged pairs of blinders
Willing to make us riders
At sea whose lives end on trees
Dangling and floating lifeless
In the air we know priceless.

My Journey Home

Having crossed this door post into my new home
Goodbye me not for my home's not a tomb
Wherein lies a poor soul whose life with lies
Was marked, sitting on the oppressed whose cries
Would they brought down such mountains on their way
Erected as pay to lead them astray;
I'd not be thus led for in such a stead
I had become the thorn that pricks their head,
A bloated balloon with nothing but air
That triggers sphincters to abscond the heir
I welcome not to defile this abode
Which to get here I've walked that uphill road
Here I lie not as in life I lied not
Now, behind I've left liars to be caught.

Only Their Reality

Death you are reality for the faithless
Not for my kind whose faith is fathomless
With your operating machine you create fear
And I fear you not for your worth I tear
And shred to bits and ribbons for bins
In which such crumbs and pieces dwell with toxins
As toxic waste none would welcome at home
Which must be filthlessly clean like pope's Rome
For those whose faith only leans on the eye
As does their stomach on a piece of pie.
My faith seeks neither for sustenance
For I'm with a Being of importance
To whom I have forfeited those shadows
After which run many men in the throes

Completing the circle

Parting as well as living tickles thoughts
Of where we end once we leave earthly ports
Yet, the life and path we choose frees from fears
And worries whether or not we'd meet spears
Or showers that bless and calm restive hearts
Whose only restfulness comes as spare parts
Unlike these hearts with large ears to gobble
The beats of a blessed heart stopped on the cross
For mankind not to be taken for dross
Without beats to echo balmy rubble
Used and abused on the mount Calvary
Whereon the blood spills wash clean this path free
Of hindrance and free my thoughts of tickle
For, with my exit I come full circle.

Here Comes the Clown

Just about to bid farewell to that clown
With a knock at my door to see me frown
Death herself sees the mistress of mystery
Who'd adorn me with a crown of misery
Then would drink from the waterless source
And would bar me the progress of my cross
Dreaming not above her shoulder, I feel
Not her icy cold hands whose chill I kill.
Many men who refuse to bear the cross?
You translate all of these men into dross!
You knocked and now think you brought me a loss?
I laugh! For my word list that's rich with plus
Has no room for frets and regrets therein
That would leave my heart without peace within.

Unwanted in this Resting Place

Even herein Morpheus's hands won't you
Let me tread along in quietude too?
When I was up your jangle sang my name
And burned tree of hope to bring on me, big shame
That your fame from which I'd rather stray
As you traded shame for disgrace as pay;
That sackcloth you would you shied away from
As your scruples lie dead by your pogrom
And won't tell your crime against blameless grime
To leave your mouth with rancid taste of lime.
Oh! Noise maker, beat your drum to defame
Where my stain free conscience yonder fans flame
To bring to you ashes that fertilized
From within my soul by God crystallized

Ebola

We knew no curse by our river
And to bring heart arrest,
You're switched to plague our nest
Flying high flags of death bringer
You're not but civilizations'
Slain and buried with no mentions.
Oh! Poor Old River
You flow not by the West
Who names you, "Killer"
For us not to know rest.
From their lab brought to you
This day in the West you nest
Far West needs samples too
To quest, "lab knowledge, the best?"

Drum by the Grave

The sounds you have just heard are the heartbeats
Of a sojourn who would his heart's drum beats
To sound the music that will leave this earth
As it will to your soul do; fill with mirth,
Giving you wings to soar above misery
Engraved on stone serve to you as History
Knowing not the gentle breeze would erode
Imprints sending through a flute a note
To raise despair's hair strands to stand on end
And thus pushed to the wall, he'd make amend
As well as revisit such stance to drag
Poor sojourner down and then stand to brag
As if equal opportunity died
Forgetting Manley Hopkins beauty pied.

www.ingramcontent.com/pod-product-compliance
Lightning Source LLC
Chambersburg PA
CBHW011718220426
43663CB00020B/2928